CW00750411

LMH OFFICIAL DICTIONARY

OF WEST INDIES
BATSMEN

Compiled by
L. Mike Henry

In the preparation of this work, we used as reference, Test Cricket Grounds: The complete guide to the world's Test cricket grounds by John Woods.

Cover Design by: Sanya Dockery
Edited by: L. M. Henry
Book Design, Layout & Typesetting by: Sanya Dockery

All pictures were taken from www.cricinfo.com and we are currently seeking permission to use said pictures.

Published by: LMH Publishing Limited
7 Norman Road,
LOJ Industrial Complex
Building 10
Kingston C.S.O., Jamaica
Tel: 876-938-0005; 938-0712
Fax: 876-759-8752
Email: lmhbookpublishing@cwjamaica.com
Website: www.lmhpublishing.com

Printed in China   ISBN 13: 978-976-8202-27-7
                                                   ISBN 10: 976-8202-27-0

CONTENTS

Introduction

The West Indies Cricket team, also known colloquially as The Windies, represents a sporting confederation of English-speaking Caribbean countries. The team is administered by the West Indies Cricket Board (WICB).

The WICB joined the sport's international ruling body, the Imperial Cricket Council, in 1926 and played their first official international match, which in cricket is called a Test, in 1928. Although blessed with some great players in their early days as a Test nation, their successes remained sporadic until the 1960s, by which time the side had changed from a white-dominated to a black-dominated side. By the 1970s, the West Indies had a side recognised as unofficial world champions, a title they retained throughout the 1980s. During these glory years, the Windies were noted for their four-man fast-bowling attack, backed up by some of the best batsmen in the world. The 1980s saw them set a then-record streak of 11 consecutive Test victories in 1984 and inflict two 5-0 "black-washes" against the old enemy of England. Throughout the 1990s and 2000s, however, West Indies cricket has declined, in part due to the rise in popularity of basketball, athletics and soccer in West Indian countries, and the team today is struggling to regain its past glory.

In their early days in the 1930s, the side represented the British colonies of the West Indies Federation plus British Guiana. The current side represents the now independent states of Antigua and Barbuda, Barbados, Dominica, Grenada, Guyana, Jamaica, St. Kitts and Nevis, St. Lucia, St. Vincent & the Grenadines and Trinidad & Tobago, and the British dependencies of Anguilla and Montserrat. National teams also exist for the various different islands, which, as they are all separate countries, very much keep their local identities and support their local favourites. These national teams take part in the West Indian first-class competition. It is also common for other international teams to play the island teams for warm-up games before they take on the combined West Indies team.

EARLY TOURS

The first international cricket played in the West Indies was between local, often predominantly white, sides and English tourists. The Middlesex player, Slade Lucas, toured Jamaica with a team in 1894-95, and two years later Arthur Priestly took a team to Barbados, Trinidad, and Jamaica, which included, for the first time, a match against a side styled "All West Indies", which the West Indians won. Lord Hawke's English team, including several English Test players, toured around the same time, playing Trinidad, Barbados and British Guiana (now Guyana). Then in 1900 the white Trinidadian Aucher Warner, the brother of future England captain Pelham Warner, led a touring side to England, but none of the matches on this tour were given first-class status. Two winters later, in 1901-2, the Hampshire wicketkeeper Richard Bennett's XI went to the West Indies, and played three games against teams styled as the "West Indies", which the hosts won 2-1. In 1904-5, Lord Brackley's XI toured the Caribbean - winning both its games against the "West Indies".

The tours to England continued in 1906 when Harold Austin led a West Indian side to England. His side played a number of county teams, and drew their game against an "England XI". However, that England XI only included one contemporary Test player - wicketkeeper Dick Lilley- and he had not been on England's most recent tour, their 1905-6 tour of South Africa. The Marylebone Cricket Club, which had taken over responsibility for arranging all official overseas England tours, visited Jamaica in 1910-11, but after that there was no international cricket of any note until the West Indian team went to England in 1923. This tour did not include a game against an England team, but there was an end-of-season game against HDG Leveson-Gower's XI against a virtual England Test side at the Scarborough cricket festival, a traditional end-of-season game against a touring side at the English seaside resort of Scarborough, which Leveson-Gower's XI won by only four wickets. 1925-26 saw another short MCC tour of Jamaica.

The MCC was eager to promote cricket throughout the British Empire, and on May 31, 1926 the West Indian Cricket Board, along with their New Zealand and Indian counterparts, was elected to the Imperial Cricket Conference (ICC), which previously consisted of the MCC and representatives of Australia and South Africa. Election to full membership of the ICC meant the West Indies could play official Test matches, which is the designation given to the most important international games, and the Windies became the fourth team actually to play a recognised Test match on June 23, 1928 when they took on England at Lord's in London. They did not, however, enjoy immediate success - the West Indies lost all three 3-day Tests in that 1928 tour by a long way, failing to score 250 runs in any of their six innings in that series. They also failed to dismiss England for under 350 runs in a series completely dominated by England.

THE EARLY TESTS (1930s AND 1940s)

The West Indies played 19 Tests in the 1930s in four series against England and one against Australia. The first four of these were played against an England team led by the Honourable Freddie Calthorpe that toured in 1929-30. However, as Harold Gilligan was leading another English team to New Zealand at exactly the same time, this was not a full-strength England side. The series ended one-all, with the West Indies first ever Test victory being recorded on February 26, 1930. West Indians George Headley scored the most runs (703) in the rubber and Learie Constantine took the most wickets (18).

The Windies toured Australia in 1930-31. They lost the Test series 4-1. The fifth and final Test showed some promise - batting first, the West Indies spent the first three days earning a 250-run lead with five wickets down in their second innings. A bold declaration was backed up by their bowlers, as Herman Griffith took four wickets and West Indies won by 30 runs to their first overseas Test victory. By the time the team left, they had left a good impression of themselves with the Australian public, although at first the team was faced with several cultural differences - for example, their hosts did not at first appreciate that the tourists' Roman Catholic beliefs would mean they would refuse to play golf on Sundays or engage in more ribald behaviour. The West Indian sides of the time were always led by white men, and the touring party to Australia comprised seven whites and eleven "natives", and the West Indian Board of Control wrote to their Australian counterparts saying "that all should reside at the same hotels". Australia at the time was implementing its "White Australia" policy, with the Australian Board having to guarantee to the Government that the non-whites would leave at the end of the tour. When the West Indians arrived in Sydney, the whites were immediately given a different hotel from the blacks. They complained, and thereafter their wishes were met. The tour lost a lot of money, part of which was down to the Great Depression then engulfing Australia. The West Indians won four and lost eight of their 14 first-class fixtures.

1933 saw another tour of England. Their hosts had just come back from defeating Australia in the infamous Bodyline series, where England's aggressive bowling at the body with a legside field attracted much criticism. England won the three-Test series of three-day Tests against the Windies 2-0. The second, drawn Test at Old Trafford, Manchester, provided an intriguing footnote to the Bodyline controversy when Manny Martindale and Learie Constantine bowled Bodyline — fast, short-pitched balls aimed at the body — against the Englishmen, the only time they faced it in international cricket. The tactic did not work, as Douglas Jardine, the English captain who ordered his players to bowl it against the Australians, did not flinch as he scored his only Test century, making 127 out of England's 374.

Another England tour of the West Indies followed in 1939. England won the first Test in Barbados on a poor pitch affected by rain, and in a match where 309 runs were scored, England took a four-wicket victory. Both sides declared one of their innings closed to have their bowlers take advantage of the poor pitch. The second Test saw the Windies win by 217 runs, and a drawn third Test saw the series go to a decider at Sabina Park in Jamaica. A massive 270 not out from George Headley saw the Windies declare on 535 for 7. Despite a century from Les Ames, England could not avoid going down by an innings and 161 runs - the West Indies had secured their first Test series victory.

The West Indies toured England in 1939. England won the first Test at Lord's easily by 8 wickets, then there was a rain-affected draw in Manchester, and finally a high-scoring draw at the Oval in mid-August. The highlight of the series for the West Indies was George Headley scoring hundreds in both innings in the Lord's Test. With the clouds of World War 11 seemingly about to envelope Europe, the rest of the tour was cancelled and the Windies returned home. They would play no more Tests until January 21, 1948 saw the start of the first Test the West Indies played since the War, which resulted in a draw against the MCC side from England. The second Test was also drawn, with George Carew and Andy Ganteaume both making centuries. Ganteaume was then dropped, ending with a Test average of 112 — the highest in Test history. The

West Indies won the final two Tests chasing sub-100 totals, and wrapped up the series 2-0, their first away-series victory.

In 1948, West Indies toured newly independent India for the first time for a five Test tour. The tour was preceded by a non-Test tour of Pakistan and followed by a similar short tour of Ceylon. After three high-scoring draws against the Indians, the West Indies wrapped up the fourth by an innings before a thrilling fifth Test, which left the Indians six runs away from victory with two wickets in hand as time ran out, so that the West Indies thus won the rubber 1-0. Carrying on from his hundred in the series against England, Everton Weekes set a record of scoring hundreds in five successive Test innings.

THE POST-WAR PERIOD (1950s)

1950 saw another tour of England, the series saw the emergence for the West Indies of their great spinning duo, Sonny Ramadhin and Alf Valentine. England won the first Test by 202 runs, but Valentine and Ramadhin's bowling would win the series for the visitors. The second Test saw the Windies put on 326 thanks to 106 from Allan Rae before Valentine (4 for 48) and Ramadhin (5 for 66) skittled England in the first innings. A mammoth 168 from Clyde Walcott saw England set a theoretical target of 601. Ramadhin's 6 for 86 and Valentine's 3 for 79 dismissed the hosts for 274. The spinning duo took 12 wickets, made 261 and Everton Weekes 129 as the third Test went the Windies way by 10 wickets, the fourth saw 14 wickets from Valentine and Ramadhin and centuries from Rae and Worrell as England were defeated by an innings. The West Indies won the series 3-1.

In 1951-52 the Windies visited Australia. The first Test saw a narrow defeat by three wickets, with the two spinners seemingly continuing their form with twelve wickets between them. The second Test was lost by seven wickets, as Australia replied to the Windies 362 and 290 with 567 (which included centuries from Lindsay Hassett and Keith Miller) and 137 for 2. 6 wickets from Worrell in the third Test saw Australia dismissed for only 82, and the Windies eventually won by six wickets to pull back to two-one down in the series. The fourth Test saw the series lost in a narrow defeat. Worrell, batting with an injured hand, scored 108 and helped the Windies to 272 before Australia made 216 in reply. 203 from the Windies left Australia a target of 260. 5 wickets from Valentine helped reduced the Aussies to 222 for 9, 38 short with 1 wicket remaining. It didn't happen, as some brilliant running between the wicket for Australia by Bill Johnston and Doug Ring saw West Indies lose their composure and the match. The fifth Test saw three batting collapses, as Australia (116 and 377) beat Windies (78 and 213) by 202 runs to finish the rubber four-one winners. The West Indies then went on to New Zealand. In the first Test encounter between the two teams, the visitors scored a five wicket victory. In the second and final Test, Alf Rae scored 99, Jeffrey Stollmeyer 152, Frank Worrell 100 and Clyde Walcott 115 as the West Indies put on 546 for 6 declared. There wasn't enough time to bowl out the opposition twice though, as the hosts made 160 and were following-on at 17 for 1 when stumps were drawn, leaving the Windies series winners.

The Indians toured at the beginning of 1953. The Windies won the second of the five Tests that were played, with the others all being draws. The highlight of these games was Frank Worrell's 237 in the fifth Test, where all the three W's scored hundreds, as the West Indies scored a 1-0 series victory. Len Hutten led an MCC (England) side to the islands in 1953-54. Sonny Ramadhin again starred for the Windies taking 23 wickets (no other West Indian took more than 8), as Walcott's 698 runs was more than 200 higher than second-placed West Indian, Everton Weekes. The five match rubber was drawn two-all.

Australia came and conquered in 1954-55. After the Aussies made 515 in the first innings of the first Test, the Windies went down by 9 wickets. Then the Windies 382 was put in the shade by 600 for 9 declared by the visitors as the second Test was drawn. A low-scoring third Test saw Australia (257 and 133 for 2) beat the hosts (182 and 207) by 8 wickets. After Australia scored 668 in the fourth Test, the series was lost, although a double century from captain Denis Atkinson and a world-record stand for the seventh wicket allowed the Windies to reach 510 and draw the Test. The fifth Test saw the West Indies win the toss and bat. Walcott's 155 was the highest score of their 357. The Australians then batted and batted, in total for 245.4 overs in the 6-day Test, as they put on 758 for 8 declared, with five players making centuries. 319 in the West Indies' second innings left them defeated by an innings and 82 runs in the Test, and by three games to nil in the series. Walcott set records by scoring five hundreds, and hundreds in both innings of a match twice. A four-Test tour of New Zealand followed in February1956. After two wins by an innings and one by 9 wickets, the

Windies were surprised by the Kiwis in the fourth, dismissing them for 145 and 77 as they recorded their first ever Test win in their 45th Test.

John Goddard returned to captain the West Indians for a five-Test tour of England in1957, which was lost three-nil, with England having the better of the two draws. Then 1957-58 Gerry Alexander led a team that defeated Pakistan three-one. It was in this series in Jamaica that Garry Sobers scored 365 not out to record what was then the highest score in Test match cricket. Alexander went on to lead the West Indies to a three-nil win over five Tests in India, and a two-one defeat to Pakistan in a three match rubber in the following winter. In 1959-60 he led as West Indies went down one-nil at home in a five-match series with England.

A PERIOD OF MIXED FORTUNES (1960s)

Despite being a country where whites are a minority, until 1960 West Indies were always captained by white cricketers, though this was more social than racial discrimination. Throughout the fifties, social theorist CLR James, the increasingly political former cricketer Learie Constantine and others called for a black captain. Constantine himself had stood in for Jackie Grant in the field against England on the 1937-38 tour, and George Headley captained the West Indies in the first Test against England in 1947-48 when the appointed, white captain, John Goddard was injured. However, no black was appointed as captain for a whole series until Frank Worrell was chosen to lead West Indies in their tour of Australia in 1960-61. In his three years as captain, Worrell moulded a bunch of talented but raw cricketers into the best team in the world.

In 1960, Australia were the best team in the world but on their way down, while West Indies were on their way up. It so happened that when they met, the two teams were of almost equal strength. The result was a series that, along with the 2005 Ashes, has been recognised as one of the greatest of all time. The first Test in Brisbane was the first Test ever to end in a tie, which in cricket means the side batting last has been dismissed with scores level. The teams shared the next two Tests. In the fourth, Australia's last pair of Ken Mackay and Lindsay Kline played out the last 100 minutes of the match to earn a draw, while Australia won the final Test and the series by two wickets. One of the days of play was attended by a world-record crowd of 90,800. Such was the impression created by Worrell's team that the newly instituted trophy for the series between the two teams was named the Frank Worrell Trophy. Half a million people lined the streets of Melbourne to bid them a ticker-tape farewell.

West Indies beat India 5-0 at home next year, and in 1963, they beat a fine English Team by three matches to one. The Lord's Test of this series saw a famous finish. With two balls left, England needed six runs to win, and West Indies one wicket. The non-striker was Colin Cowdery, who had his left arm in a sling, having fractured it earlier in the day. However, David Allen safely played out the last two balls and the match ended in a draw. Worrell retired at the end of the series. The selectors picked Garry Sobers to succeed him.

Worrell did, however, serve as the team manager when

West Indies hosted Australia in 1964-65. The matches against Australia were bitterly fought, with accusations about Charlie Griffith's action (he was accused of throwing, which is banned in the laws of cricket) and bouncer wars. The West Indies won this series 2-1 to be the unofficial world champions. Sobers was not as good at man-management as Worrell and cracks soon began to appear. Often it was his individual brilliance that made the difference between a win and a loss. Throughout the sixties, West Indies bowling was led by Wes Hall, Griffith, Lance Gibbs and Sobers himself. Hall and Griffith faded and then retired by the end of the decade, but WI could find no replacement for them till the mid-seventies.

Sobers was at his best in England in 1966, scoring 722 runs and taking 20 wickets in the five Tests. Three times he topped 150, and the 163 at Lord's turned a certain defeat into a near victory. West Indies won 3-1. England toured the West Indies in 1967-68 for a series that became noted for England's deliberate slow play. West Indies were forced to follow on in the first Test but saved it without difficulty. The second Test was played on an underprepared wicket at Kingston. England won an important toss and scored 376. The bounce of the wicket having become very uneven, West Indies collapsed to 143 and followed on again. On the fourth day in the second innings, a disputed decision led to a crowd riot, and the match had to be stopped for some time. In a curious decision, the West Indian Cricket Board (WICB) agreed to add a 75-minute sixth day to compensate for the lost time. Sobers played an outstanding innings of 113 not out, which allowed West Indies to set England a target of 159 in 155 minutes.

England just about saved the game, losing eight wickets for 68. In the fourth Test, West Indies gained a first innings lead of 122 at Port-of-Spain, but with the second innings score at 92 for 2, Sobers, frustrated by England's slow over rates and wanting to give himself a chance, albeit a small one, to win, surprisingly declared the innings, a decision for which he was widely criticised at the time. England were set a target of 215 in 165 minutes and they achieved it with 3 minutes to spare. West Indies made one last effort to win the final Test, but England drew it with only wicket left in their second innings. West Indies lost the series 0-1, the first defeat since 1960-61.

Australia and Bill Lawry had their revenge in 1968-69, when West Indies lost the series, which was played in Australia, 1-3. New Zealand managed to draw the series that followed, and then in 1969 West Indies were defeated 0-2 in England.

A PERIOD OF WORLD DOMINANCE (1970s)

West Indies' woes overflowed into the seventies. At home in 1970-71, they lost to India for the first time. In the next year, a five Test series against New Zealand cricket team ended with no team coming close to winning one. The problem was that Sobers was the only world-class bowler in the side. A major find in the New Zealand series was Lawrence Rowe, who started off with a double century and century on his debut. Under Rohan Kanhai's captaincy, West Indies showed the first signs of revival. Australia won the closely fought 1972-73 series in the Caribbean by two Tests. With Sobers back - but Kanhai still the captain - West Indies defeated England 2-0 in 1973, which included a win by an innings and 226 runs at Lord's, their biggest win against England. The return series in West Indies ended 1-1, though the home team was the better side. Rowe continued his run, scoring three centuries including a 302 at Kingston. The final Test of this 1973-74 series marked the end of an era in West Indies cricket - it was the last Test of both Garry Sobers and Rohan Kanhai, and marked the emergence of fast bowler Andy Roberts.

The new captain Clive Lloyd had made his first appearance in Test cricket in 1966 and had since become a fixture in the side. His avuncular, bespectacled appearance and a stoop near the shoulders masked the fact that he was a very fine fielder, especially in the covers, and a devastating stroke player. Lloyd's first assignment was the tour of India in 1974-75. West Indies won the first two Tests against India comfortably. Greenidge started his career with 107 and 93 on his debut. Richards failed in his first Test, but scored 192 in his second. India fought back to win the next two, but Lloyd hit 242 in the final Test to win the series.

West Indies won the inaugural World Cup in England in 1975, defeating Australia in the final. Then in 1975-76 they toured Australia, only to lose 1-5 in the six-Test series, and then beat India at home two-one in a four Test series later that same winter. It was in 1975-76 that quick bowler Michael Holding made his debut. Colin Croft and Joel Garner made their debut the next year, and Malcolm Marshall two years after. In the span of about four years, West Indies brought together a bowling line-up of a quality that had rarely been seen before. The Indian tour saw the debut of Vivian

Richards, arguably the finest West Indian batsman ever, and Gordon Greenidge, who joined a strong batting line-up that already included Alvin Kallicharan and opener Roy Fredericks in addition to Rowe and Lloyd. These players formed the nucleus of the side that became recognised as world Test match champions until the beginning of the 1990s.

Next came a tour of England in 1976. In a TV interview before the series, English captain Tony Greig commented that the West Indies tend to do badly under pressure and that "we'll make them grovel". This comment, especially as it came from a South African-born player, touched a raw nerve of the West Indians. Throughout the series, the English batsmen were subjected to some very hostile bowling. After the first two Tests ended in draws, West Indies won the next three. Of the many heroes for West Indies, Richards stood out with 829 runs in four Tests. He hit 232 at Trent Bridge and 291 at the Oval. Greenidge scored three hundreds, two of which were on the difficult wicket at Old Trafford. Roberts and Holding shared 55 wickets between them, Holding's 8 for 92 and 6 for 57 on the dead wicket at the Oval being a superlative effort.

West Indies won a home series against a tough Pakistan side in 1976-77. A few months later, the World Series Cricket (WSC) controversy broke out. Most of the West Indian players signed up with Kerry Packer, an Australian TV magnate who was attempting to set up his own international cricket competition. The Australian team that toured West Indies the next year included no Packer players, but West Indies Cricket Board fielded a full-strength team under the argument that none of the West Indies players had refused to play, but disputes arose in the matter of payment and about the selection of certain players. Before the third Test, Lloyd resigned his captaincy. Within two days all the other WSC-contracted players also withdrew. Alvin Kallicharran captained the team for the remaining Tests of the series, which the Windies won three-one.

WICB allowed the WSC players to appear in the 1979 World Cup, and the West Indies retained the title with little difficulty. By the end of 1979, the WSC disputes were resolved. Kallicharran was deposed after losing a six-match series one-nil in India and Lloyd returned as captain for a tour against a full-strength Australia (where the Windies won two-nil, with one draw) and New Zealand. The latter tour was full of controversy. New Zealand won the first Test at Dunedin by one wicket, but West Indies were never happy with the umpiring. West Indian discontent boiled over the next Test at Christchurch. While running into bowl, Colin Croft deliberately shouldered the umpire Fred Goodall. When Goodall went to talk to Lloyd about Croft's behaviour, he had to walk all the way to meet the West Indian captain, as the latter did not move an inch from his position at the slips. After tea on the third day, West Indies refused to take the field unless Goodall was removed. They were persuaded to continue, and it took intense negotiations between the two boards to keep the tour on track. The Kiwis won the three match series after the second and third Tests ended in draws.

A PERIOD OF TURBULENCE (1980s)

The 1980s started with a one-nil victory away to England over five Tests, one-nil away to Pakistan over four Tests, two-nil home to England over four Tests and a one-all draw away to Australia. Then in 1982-83, a West Indian rebel team toured apartheid South Africa. It was led by Lawrence Rowe and included prominent players like Alvin Kallicharan, Colin Croft, Collis King and Sylvester Clarke. WICB banned the players for life (which was later revoked), and some were refused entry back home. However,

WI Test series in the 1980s						
SEASON	Vs	HOSTS	P	W	L	D
1979-80	NZ	NZ	3	0	1	2
1980	ENG	ENG	5	1	0	4
1980-81	PAK	PAK	4	1	0	3
1980-81	ENG	WI	4	2	0	2
1981-82	AUS	AUS	3	1	1	1
1982-83	IND	WI	5	2	0	3
1983-84	IND	IND	6	3	0	3
1983-84	AUS	WI	4	3	0	1
1984	ENG	ENG	5	5	0	0
1984-85	AUS	AUS	5	3	1	1
1983-84	AUS	WI	1	0	0	1
1984-85	NZ	WI	4	2	0	2
1985-86	ENG	WI	5	5	0	0
1986-87	PAK	PAK	3	1	1	1
1986-87	NZ	NZ	3	1	1	1
1987-88	IND	IND	4	1	1	2
1987-88	PAK	WI	3	1	1	1
1988	ENG	ENG	5	4	0	1
1988-89	AUS	AUS	5	3	1	1
1988-89	IND	WI	4	3	0	1
1989-90	ENG	WI	4	2	1	1

After losing their first series of the 1980s in March 1980, the West Indies went throughout the rest of the decade undefeated.

the rebels managed another tour the next year, which included most of the players of the original team. Despite this loss of talent, the official Windies side continued to dominate. In the period to 1985-86 they won every series they played, with their only notable defeat being in the one-day arena, when, to general surprise, they lost to India in the final of the 1983 World Cup. The winning streak included two five-nil victories over England in five-Test series, which became known as the black-washes.

During this streak the West Indian captain Llyod retired from Test cricket at the end of the 1984-85 series against Australia. In total Lloyd had captained West Indies in 74 Test matches, winning 36 of them. Vivian Richards was Lloyd's successor, and continued the run of success. Meanwhile, a change of the old guard was also happening. Joel Garner and Michael Holding had retired by 1987. A major find was Curtly Ambrose, who was as tall as Garner and as equally effective with the ball. Courtney Walsh, who made his first appearance in 1984, bowled with an action that resembled Holding. Ian Bishop also had a similar action, and was as good a bowler till injuries inter-rupted his career. Patrick Patterson was faster than all the rest, but had a short career. Marshall still was the finest fast bowler in the world. Batting was beginning to show signs of weakness. When West Indies failed in the 1986-87 World Series Cup , it was only the second time (after the 1983 World Cup) that they had failed to win a one-day tournament or series that they took part in. They also failed to qualify for the semifinal of the 1987 World Cup. By the end of the eighties, while still the best team in the world, they had lost the aura of invincibility that they had till the middle of the decade. Finding good replacements for senior players was again becoming a problem.

FALL FROM GRACE

It was five more years before West Indies lost a series, but they had a number of close shaves. South Africa on their comeback played its first Test match in Bridgetown, a match which was attended by less than 10,000 people because of a boycott. Needing 201 to win on the last day, South Africa reached 123 for 2 before Curtly Ambrose and Courtney Walsh took the remaining wickets for 25 runs. In 1992-93, West Indies defeated Australia by one run at Adelaide, where a loss could have cost them the series. In 1992, West Indies once again failed to qualify for the World Cup semifinal. Australia finally defeated West Indies 2-1 in 1994-95 to become the unofficial world champions of Test cricket. The 1996 World Cup ended with a defeat in the semifinal, which forced Richie Richardson, who had taken over the captaincy from Richards in 1991, to end his career. West Indies made their first-ever official tour to South Africa in 1998-99. It ended in disaster, starting with player revolts and ending with a 0-5 defeat. The 1999 World Cup campaign ended in the group stages. The next year, England won a series against West Indies for the first time in thirty-one years. West Indies ended the decade with another 0-5 defeat in Australia.

For most of the nineties and afterwards, the West Indian batting has been dominated by Brian Lara. He became a regular in the side after the retirement of Richards in 1991. Against England at Antigua 1993-94, he scored 375 and broke Sobers' world record for the highest individual score in Test cricket. He continued his fine form for Warickshire and hit seven first-class hundreds in eight innings. The last of these was a 501 not out against Durham, which improved upon Hanif Mohammed's thirty-five-year-old record as the highest score in first-class cricket. Bowling support was given by Curtly Ambrose and Courtney Walsh, the latter after setting a then world record of 519 wickets. However, these two were gone by 2001. The bowlers to follow had big shoes to fill (quite literally) and ultimately have not responded close to the level that Ambrose and Walsh have set. Despite the presence of some good batsmen like Shivnarine Chanderpaul and Ramnaresh Sarwan, Brian Lara still remained the crucial figure of the side.

After a two-nil defeat to New Zealand in 1999-00, Lara was replaced as captain by Jimmy Adams, who initially enjoyed series wins against Zimbabwe and Pakistan, but a three-one defeat to England and a five-nil whitewash by Austrailia saw him replaced by Carl Hooper for the 2000-01 visit by South Africa. By the time Lara was restored to the captaincy in 2002-03 series had been lost to South Africa, Sri Lanka, Pakistan, New Zealand and India. The only series win of note was against India (although Zimbabwe and Bangladesh were still beaten) as the West Indies plummeted to eighth place in the world-rankings, below all the other established Test nations.

After losing his first series of his second captaincy period to world-champions Australia, Lara secured success against Sri Lanka and Zimbabwe, before another poor run saw three-nil defeats over four Tests against both South Africa and England, although the fourth Test against England was drawn after Lara posted a world-record individual Test score of 400 not out. The West Indies were then whitewashed four-nil in England. Lara's last act as captain was to win the 2004 ICC Champions Trophy, a one-day competition second only to the Cricket World Cup, at the Oval, London — a win that was a welcome surprise for the Caribbean which had just been hit by Hurricane Ivan.

This joy was short-lived as a major dispute broke out in 2005 between the West Indian Players Association (WIPA) and the Cricket Board. The point of contention was the 'clause 5' of the tour contract which gave WICB the sole and exclusive right to arrange for sponsorship, advertising, licensing, merchandising and promotional activities relating to WICB or any WICB Team. Digicel were the sponsors of the West Indian Team, while most of the players had contracts with Cable & Wireless. This and a payment dispute meant the West Indies first announced a team absent Lara and a number of other leading West Indians for South Africa's visit in 2004-05, leading to Shivnarine becoming captain. Some of these players did, in the end, compete. The dispute had not been finally resolved, though, and rumbled on, leading to a second-string side being named for the tour of Sri Lanka in 2005. The dispute was not resolved until October 2005, when a full-strength side was finally named for the 2005-6 tour of Australia. It was on this tour that Brian Lara overtook Australian Allan Border as the highest run-scorer in Test match cricket but lost the series 0-3.

TOURNAMENT HISTORY

World Cup

- 1975: Won
- 1979: Won
- 1983: Runners up
- 1987: First round
- 1992: 6th place
- 1996: Semi Finals
- 1999: First round
- 2003: First round

ICC Champions Trophy

- 2002: First round
- 2004: Won
- 2006: Runners up

ICC Knockout

- 1998: Runners up
- 2000: First round

All statistics are up to date to the end of
November 2006

JAMES ADAMS
(Jamaica)

Born January 9, 1968

Batting style:
Left-handed bat

James Clive Adams was a steady left-handed batsman who had a spectacular start to his Test career. After 12 Tests, only Australian batting great Sir Donald Bradman had a better record in the history of Test cricket than his 1132 runs at 87. In the mid-'90s, however, he suffered a crisis of confidence, a problem that may have stemmed from an unfortunate incident on the 1995 tour of England. Batting in fading light, Adams ducked into a bouncer from Somerset's Andre van Troost, shattering his cheekbone. An increasingly defensive player, especially when facing spin, he proved just as negative in his tactics when appointed captain in 2000. His tenure started well with four wins and two draws in his first six games, but thereafter a weak side lost their way and he lost seven of his next eight matches, culminating in a 5-0 whitewash in Australia. That tour marked the end of his Test career.

BATTING AND FIELDING AVERAGES

					Test Career							
mat	inns	no	runs	hs	ave	bf	sr	100	50	4s	6s	ct/st
54	90	17	3010	208	41.23			6	14			48
					One Day International							
127	105	28	2204	82	28.62		-		14			-

F. C. M. ALEXANDER
(Jamaica)

Born November 2, 1928

Batting style:
Right-handed bat

Franz Copeland Murray Alexander was a popular captain whose initial selection for the 1957 tour of England was far from popular. Alexander had experience of the conditions - he was a Cambridge Blue in 1952 and 1953 - but it was felt there were better keepers in the Caribbean. He struggled, and his retention in the side caused further dismay, as did his appointment as Frank Worrell's successor as captain. But he rose to the challenge, leading by example, before stepping aside when Worrell returned. Relieved of the captaincy, his batting blossomed and in Australia in 1960-61 he scored at least a half-century in every Test, heading the averages with 484 runs at 60.50. He was also a football Blue, and he won an England amateur cap and an FA Amateur Cup winner's medal. A veterinary surgeon, he retired after the 1960-61 tour.

BATTING AND FIELDING AVERAGES

Test Career

mat	inns	no	runs	hs	ave	bf	sr	100	50	4s	6s	ct	st
25	38	6	961	108	30.03				1	7			85	5

One Day International

127	105	28	2204	82	28.62		-	14			-

KEITH ARTHURTON
(Nevis)

Born January 9, 1968

Batting style:
Left-handed bat

Only the third Test player from the small island of Nevis, Arthurton's best career moments were an unbeaten 157 at Brisbane in 1992-93, a century against England in Jamaica in 1993-94, and a flurry of strutting seventies.

BATTING AND FIELDING AVERAGES

						Test Career								
mat	inns	no	runs	hs	ave	bf	sr	100	50	4s	6s	ct	st
33	50	5	1382	157	30.71			2	8			22	
						One Day International								
105	93	20	1904	84	26.08		-		9			27	

BASIL BUTCHER
(Guyana -then British Guiana)

Born September 3, 1933

Batting style:
Right-handed bat

A supple, wristy, resolute batsman, Basil Butcher became a consistently reliable performer at No. 4 or 5 in the West Indies order. In his first Test series, against India in 1958-59, he made 486 runs at 69.42, but had a checkered career thereafter, until the 1963 tour of England, when he made 383 runs in eight completed innings, including 133 out of 229 in the memorable draw at Lord's.

BATTING AND FIELDING AVERAGES

Test Career

mat	inns	no	runs	hs	ave	bf	sr	100	50	4s	6s	ct	st
98	145	29	1439	53	12.40		-		1			18	

One Day International

mat	inns	no	runs	hs	ave	bf	sr	100	50	4s	6s	ct	st
176	96	36	639	31	28.62		-	-				45	

SHERWIN CAMPBELL
(Barbados)

Born November 1, 1970

**Batting style:
Right-hand bat**

Given their problems of finding a stable opening pair, it seems strange that the West Indies couldn't find a place for the dashing Sherwin Campbell. He was dropped after their disastrous tour of Australia in 2000-01.

BATTING AND FIELDING AVERAGES

mat	inns	no	runs	hs	ave	bf	sr	100	50	4s	6s	ct	st
Test Career													
52	93	4	2882	208	32.38	7159	40.25	4	18	373	9	47	0
One Day International													
90	87	0	2283	105	26.24	3853	59.25	2	14	207	7	23	0
First Class													
177	316	22	10873	211	36.98			26	55			164	0
List A													
175	171	4	4403	105	26.36			3	27			58	0

SHIVNARINE CHANDERPAUL
(Guyana)

Born August 16, 1974

Batting style:
Left-hand bat

Shivnarine Chanderpaul captained the West Indies in fourteen Tests and sixteen one-day internationals. The left-handed Chanderpaul is known for his doggedness and ability to stick on the wicket for long hours. His very unorthodox stance while batting is also highly recognised as one of the "crabbiest" techniques in international cricket, with his body almost directly facing the bowler.

Chanderpaul made his first Test century in his 19th Test match - after having scored 15 half-centuries in the preceding 18 matches. In the third of a five-Test series against India in 1996-97, he made 137 not out at the Kensington Oval in Bridgetown, Barbados. He also featured with his Guyanese counterpart, Ramnaresh Sarwan, making 104 in chasing a world record 418 to win in the fourth innings of the final Test match versus Australia in 2002-03.

Chanderpaul's best first class score is 303 not out versus Jamaica for Guyana, and, despite his reputation as a dogged batsman, he has also made the third fastest century in Test cricket, scoring three figures in just 67 balls at the GCC Ground Bourda, Guyana, also in the 2002-03 series against Australia.

BATTING AND FIELDING AVERAGES

mat	inns	no	runs	hs	ave	bf	sr	100	50	4s	6s	ct	st
Test Career													
101	173	22	6736	203	44.60	15634	43.08	14	40	785	16	44	0
One Day International													
205	193	25	6229	150	37.07	8843	70.43	4	43	546	53	59	0
20/20 Int.													
1	1	0	26	26	26.00	27	96.29	0	0	2	0	1	0
First-Class													
201	328	53	14087	303	51.22			39	68			123	0
List A													
296	276	42	8995	150	38.44			5	64			92	0
20/20													
1	1	0	26	26	26.00	27	96.29	0	0			1	0

ROBERT CHRISTIANI
(Guyana – then British Guiana)

Born July 19, 1920

**Batting style:
Right-hand bat**

A modest average of 26.35 in 22 Tests for the West Indies between 1948 and 1954, concealed a player of nimble footwork and a positive and altogether joyful approach to the game whose slim, boyish physique and ever-present spectacles simply added to his appeal. His overall first-class record - 5,103 runs at 40.50 with 12 hundreds - more accurately reflected his ability.

BATTING AND FIELDING AVERAGES

Test Career

mat	inns	no	runs	hs	ave	bf	sr	100	50	4s	6s	ct	st
22	37	3	896	107	26.35			1	4		2	19	2

First-Class

mat	inns	no	runs	hs	ave	bf	sr	100	50	4s	6s	ct	st
88	142	16	5103	181	40.50			12	27			96	12

JEFF DUJON
(Jamaica)

Born May 28, 1956

Batting style:
Right-hand bat

Peter Jeffrey Leroy (Jeff) Dujon was the wicketkeeper for the West Indies cricket team of the 1980s, an athletic presence behind the stumps as well as a competent lower-order batsman.

Dujon made his first-class debut in 1974, going on to play 200 first-class matches for Jamaica and the West Indies in a career that lasted nineteen years. He scored nearly 10,000 runs at an average approaching 40 runs per innings, an impressive statistic when compared to other specialist wicketkeepers over time, as well as completing 447 catches and 22 stumpings.

Dujon was one of five Wisden Cricketers of the Year in 1989 and since retiring as a player in 1992, has worked as assistant coach to the West Indies national team and in development of young cricket players in his native Jamaica.

cont'd.

BATTING AND FIELDING AVERAGES

									Test Career					
mat	inns	no	runs	hs	ave	bf	sr	100	50	4s	6s	ct	st
81	115	11	3322	139	31.94			5	16		11	267	5

One Day International													
169	120	36	1945	82	23.15	2881	67.51	0	6			183	21

First-Class													
200	298	48	9763	163	39.05			21	50			447	22

List A													
211	160	43	2694	97	23.02			0	12			218	27

DAREN GANGA
(Trinidad)

Born January 14, 1979

Batting style:
Right-hand bat

Daren Ganga is a right-handed batsman and a right-arm off-break bowler. He has captained the Trinidad and Tobago cricket team, the West Indies A team and the West Indies Under-23 team.

Having had a steady, but unspectacular tour of Australia in 2000/01, he didn't manage to really make his mark until a set of back-to-back centuries against Australia.

In July 2005, he was voted Trinidad and Tobago's Cricketer of the Year following a successful Carib Beer competition, during which, in a match against the Leeward Islands, he scored 265 runs in a single innings. In April 2006 he was one of six players shortlisted for the captaincy of the West Indies cricket team.

cont'd.

BATTING AND FIELDING AVERAGES

Test Career

mat	inns	no	runs	hs	ave	bf	sr	100	50	4s	6s	ct	st
41	72	1	1938	135	27.29	4910	39.47	3	9	259	2	25	0

One Day International

mat	inns	no	runs	hs	ave	bf	sr	100	50	4s	6s	ct	st
35	34	1	843	71	25.54	1414	83.87	0	9	69	7	11	0

20/20 Int.

mat	inns	no	runs	hs	ave	bf	sr	100	50	4s	6s	ct	st
1	1	0	26	26	26.00	31	83.87	0	0	3	1	0	0

First-Class

mat	inns	no	runs	hs	ave	bf	sr	100	50	4s	6s	ct	st
126	219	16	7322	265	36.06			17	35			80	0

List A

mat	inns	no	runs	hs	ave	bf	sr	100	50	4s	6s	ct	st
81	80	7	2035	101	27.87			2	16			27	0

20/20

mat	inns	no	runs	hs	ave	bf	sr	100	50	4s	6s	ct	st
6	6	2	159	62	39.75	124	128.22	0	1			3	0

CHRIS GAYLE
(Jamaica)

Born September 21, 1979

Batting style:
Left-hand bat

Christopher (Chris) Henry Gayle played for the West Indies at youth international level after he made his first-class debut aged 19 for Jamaica. He played his first one-day international 11 months later, and his first Test match 6 months after that.

Gayle, who normally opens the innings when he plays for the West Indies, is a destructive batsman who is most effective playing square of the wicket. In July 2001, Gayle (175), together with Daren Ganga (89), established the record for opening partnerships at Queens Sports Club, Bulawayo, when they put on 214 together against Zimbabwe.

cont'd.

BATTING AND FIELDING AVERAGES

Test Career

mat	inns	no	runs	hs	ave	bf	sr	100	50	4s	6s	ct	st
64	113	3	4259	317	38.71	7224	55.73	7	26	673	31	66	0

One Day International

155	152	9	5633	153	39.39	6281	80.03	15	28	686	83	74	0

20/20 Int.

1	1	0	10	10	10.00	12	83.33	0	0	2	0	0	0

First-class

133	238	16	9769	317	44.00			22	51			122	0

List A

202	199	15	7414	153	40.29			17	40			91	0

20/20

5	4	1	97	40	32.33	75	129.33	0	0			2	0

JOHN GODDARD
(Barbados)

Born April 21, 1919

Batting style:
Left-hand bat

John Douglas Claude Goddard was a cricketer and one-time captain of the West Indies Test side. He captained the West Indian team through several tours, including West Indies' maiden tours of India and New Zealand. His first stretch as a captain started in the late 1940s and lasted five series. The West Indies won eight and drew five out of 17 matches.

BATTING AND FIELDING AVERAGES

Test Career

mat	inns	no	runs	hs	ave	bf	sr	100	50	4s	6s	ct	st
27	39	11	859	83	30.67			0	4		1	22	0

First-class

mat	inns	no	runs	hs	ave	bf	sr	100	50	4s	6s	ct	st
111	145	32	3769	218	33.35			5	17			94	0

LARRY GOMES
(Trinidad)

Born July 13, 1953

Batting style:
Left-hand bat

Larry Gomes was a slightly built, upright, elegant and efficient batsman in times of strife rather than an exuberant destroyer. Six centuries against Australia, none better than that on a bouncy Perth strip in 1984 that set up an innings victory, tell their own tale of a quiet achiever.

BATTING AND FIELDING AVERAGES

Test Career

mat	inns	no	runs	hs	ave	bf	sr	100	50	4s	6s	ct	st
60	91	11	3171	143	39.63			9	13		2	18	0

One Day International

83	64	15	1415	101	28.87	2578	54.88	1	6			14	0

First-class

231	370	50	12982	200	40.56			32	63			77	0

List A

156	132	24	3115	103	28.84			2	13			34	0

GERRY GOMEZ
(Trinidad)

Born October 10, 1919

Batting style:
Right-hand bat

Gerald Ethridge Gomez died from a heart attack when playing tennis in Trinidad on August 6, 1996, aged 76. He made his name as a batsman, scoring 161 not out for Trinidad against Jamaica when he was still a teenager, and earning selection for the 1939 tour of England, though his achievements there did not match his promise.

BATTING AND FIELDING AVERAGES

Test Career

mat	inns	no	runs	hs	ave	bf	sr	100	50	4s	6s	ct	st
29	46	5	1243	101	30.31			1	8		0	18	0

First-Class

| 126 | 182 | 27 | 6764 | 216 | 43.63 | | | 14 | 29 | | | 92 | 0 |

GORDON GREENIDGE
(Barbados)

Born May 1, 1951

Batting style:
Right-hand bat

Cuthbert Gordon Greenidge was a feared batsman for the West Indies. He began his Test career in 1974 and continued playing internationally until 1991. He was half of the West Indies' most prolific opening partnership with Desmond Haynes. Greenidge went on to play 108 Test matches scoring 7,558 runs with 19 centuries. He also played 128 one day internationals, including the 1975 and 1983 World Cup Finals, scoring 5,134 runs and 11 centuries.

Greenidge is perhaps best known in England for his amazing double-double century performances against the home side in the 1984 summer Test series (also known as the "Blackwash" series WI winning 5-0). He scored 214 runs during the second Test at Lords in June of 1984, then followed up with 223 runs during the fourth Test at Old Trafford during the last five days of July, cementing his place in Test cricket history.

BATTING AND FIELDING AVERAGES

Test Career

mat	inns	no	runs	hs	ave	bf	sr	100	50	4s	6s	ct	st
108	185	16	7558	226	44.72			19	34		67	96	0

One Day International

| 128 | 127 | 13 | 5134 | 133 | 45.03 | 7908 | 64.92 | 11 | 31 | | | 45 | 0 |

First-Class

| 523 | 889 | 75 | 37354 | 273 | 45.88 | | | 92 | 183 | | | 516 | 0 |

List A

| 440 | 436 | 33 | 16349 | 186 | 40.56 | | | 33 | 94 | | | 172 | 0 |

CHARLIE GRIFFITH
(Barbados)

Born December 14, 1938

Batting Style:
Right-hand bat

Charles Christopher Griffith is a former West Indian cricketer who played in 28 Tests from 1960 to 1969. He was a Wisden Cricketer of the Year in 1964.

BATTING AND FIELDING AVERAGES

Test Career

mat	inns	no	runs	hs	ave	bf	sr	100	50	4s	6s	ct	st
28	42	10	530	54	16.56			0	1		4	16	0

First-class

mat	inns	no	runs	hs	ave	bf	sr	100	50	4s	6s	ct	st
96	119	32	1502	98	17.26			0	4			39	0

List A

mat	inns	no	runs	hs	ave	bf	sr	100	50	4s	6s	ct	st
2	0	0	0	0	-	0	-	0	0	0	0	1	0

GEORGE HEADLEY
(Panama)

Born May 30, 1909

Batting Style:
Right-hand bat

George Headley, born in Panama, died November 30, 1983 in Kingston, Jamaica. He was taken to Jamaica at the age of ten and went on to become the finest West Indian batsman of the 1930s and 1940s. He has a career batting average in Test cricket of an exceptional 60.83, the third highest of any player and behind only Sir Donald Bradman and Graeme Pollock.

Headley played mainly off of the back foot, yet he was an attacking batsman; a fine cutter and a powerful driver. He played in the first ever Test match on West Indian soil in 1929/30 and went on to score an exceptional aggregate of 703 runs in the series at an average of 87.87, including four centuries. In 1948 he became the first black man to captain the West Indies, and in his final appearance in January 1954 he set a record as the oldest West Indian Test cricketer (44 years and 236 days) which is unlikely to be beaten.

BATTING AND FIELDING AVERAGES

Test Career

mat	inns	no	runs	hs	ave	bf	sr	100	50	4s	6s	ct	st
22	40	4	2190	270	60.83			10	5		1	14	0

First-Class

mat	inns	no	runs	hs	ave	bf	sr	100	50	4s	6s	ct	st
103	164	22	9921	344	69.86			33	44			76	0

WAVELL HINDS
(Jamaica)

Born September 7, 1976

Batting style:
Left-hand bat

Wavell Wayne Hinds is currently a member of the West Indian cricket team at Test and one-day international level.

He is an aggressive left-handed batsman and useful right-arm medium pace bowler who made his Test debut against Zimbabwe in 2000. He scored 165 in just his fourth Test match against Pakistan and has a highest Test score of 213.

Hinds has struggled to hold down a regular place in the West Indies team due to team changes and poor form.

BATTING AND FIELDING AVERAGES

Test Career

mat	inns	no	runs	hs	ave	bf	sr	100	50	4s	6s	ct	st
45	80	1	2608	213	33.01	5459	47.77	5	14	368	16	32	0

One Day International

mat	inns	no	runs	hs	ave	bf	sr	100	50	4s	6s	ct	st
114	107	9	2835	127	28.92	4292	66.05	5	14	258	49	28	0

Twenty20 Int.

mat	inns	no	runs	hs	ave	bf	sr	100	50	4s	6s	ct	st
1	1	0	14	14	14.00	18	77.77	0	0	1	0	0	0

First-class

mat	inns	no	runs	hs	ave	bf	sr	100	50	4s	6s	ct	st
119	204	6	6715	213	33.91			17	30			60	0

List A

mat	inns	no	runs	hs	ave	bf	sr	100	50	4s	6s	ct	st
181	170	14	4423	127	28.35			6	22			43	0

Twenty20

mat	inns	no	runs	hs	ave	bf	sr	100	50	4s	6s	ct	st
3	2	0	58	44	58.00	51	113.72	0	0			0	0

VANBURN HOLDER
(Barbados)

Born October 10, 1945

Batting Style:
Right-hand bat

Vanburn Alonzo Holder is a former West Indian cricketer who played in forty Tests and twelve ODIs from 1969 to 1979.

BATTING AND FIELDING AVERAGES

	mat	inns	no	runs	hs	ave	bf	sr	100	50	4s	6s	ct	st
Test Career														
	40	59	11	682	42	14.20			0	0		8	16	0
One Day International														
	12	6	1	64	30	12.80	85	75.29	0	0	4	2	6	0
First-Class														
	313	358	81	3593	122	12.97			1	4			99	0
List A														
	196	109	35	587	35	7.93			0	0			46	0

DAVID HOLFORD
(Barbados)

Born April 16, 1940

Batting Style:
Right-hand bat

An allrounder, **David Holford** was a handy lower-order batsman and a tidy legspinner. In his second Test at Lord's in 1966, he saved the match by adding 274 for the sixth wicket with Garry Sobers, his cousin. Much was expected of him, but in 1968 he was struck down with pleurisy and he was never quite the same player again. Holford's 105 there was his sole Test century, and he only managed one five-for as well, a matchwinning effort against India in Barbados nearly ten years later. In 1977 he was a surprising recruit for Kerry Packer's World Series in 1977.

BATTING AND FIELDING AVERAGES

Test Career

mat	inns	no	runs	hs	ave	bf	sr	100	50	4s	6s	ct	st
24	39	5	768	105	22.58			1	3		1	18	0

First-Class

99	149	27	3821	111	31.31			3	20			83	0

List A

12	9	2	135	46	19.28			0	0			4	0

CARL HOOPER
(Guyana)

Born December 15, 1966

Batting Style:
Right-hand bat

Carl Llewellyn Hooper was renowned for his exquisite batting style. His highest innings score of 233 was made during a Test series in India in 2001. He has made 5762 runs in his Test cricket career. Hooper could be an erratic Test batsman, as his low average of 36.46 over 102 Tests shows. In ODI play, Hooper's aggressive style of batting did not seem to translate to success as again, he only averaged 35.74 off 227 matches.

Despite his lower than perhaps expected average, Hooper holds the accolade of being the only cricketer in the world to have scored 5000 runs, taken 100 wickets, 100 catches and received 100 caps in both ODIs and Tests.

cont'd.

BATTING AND FIELDING AVERAGES

Test Career

mat	inns	no	runs	hs	ave	bf	sr	100	50	4s	6s	ct	st
102	173	15	5762	233	36.46	11462	50.27	13	27	633	63	115	0

One Day International

| 227 | 206 | 43 | 5761 | 113 | 35.34 | 7517 | 76.63 | 7 | 29 | 409 | 65 | 120 | 0 |

First-Class

| 339 | 535 | 52 | 23034 | 236 | 47.68 | | | 69 | 104 | | | 375 | 0 |

List A

| 457 | 414 | 81 | 13357 | 145 | 40.11 | | | 15 | 85 | | | 242 | 0 |

Twenty20

| 10 | 9 | 2 | 162 | 49 | 23.14 | 156 | 103.84 | 0 | 0 | | | 6 | 0 |

BOWLING AVERAGES

Test Career

mat	balls	runs	wkts	bbi	bbm	ave	econ	sr	4	5	10
102	13794	5635	114	5/26	7/178	49.42	2.45	121.00	1	4	0

One Day International

| 227 | 9573 | 6958 | 193 | 4/34 | 4/34 | 36.05 | 4.36 | 49.60 | 3 | 0 | 0 |

First-Class

| 339 | 46464 | 19595 | 555 | 7/93 | | 35.30 | 2.53 | 83.71 | | 18 | 0 |

List A

| 457 | 19718 | 13611 | 396 | 5/41 | 5/41 | 34.37 | 4.14 | 49.79 | 5 | 1 | 0 |

Twenty20

| 10 | 204 | 197 | 8 | 4/18 | 4/18 | 24.62 | 5.79 | 25.50 | 1 | 0 | 0 |

CONRAD HUNTE
(Barbados)

Born May 9, 1932

Batting Style:
Right-hand bat

Sir Conrad Cleophas Hunte died of a heart attack after playing tennis in Sydney on December 3, 1999, aged 67. Conrad Hunte was one of the greatest West Indian batsmen of a great generation; he also played a major role in the reconstruction of South African cricket, and was a figure of moral authority in the wider world. As a batsman, Hunte could match anyone stroke-for-stroke, especially on the leg side, if he wanted. But he subdued his attacking nature in Test cricket to let his team-mates play their shots, a decision which was vital in making the West Indian side of the early 1960s one of the most complete of all time.

BATTING AND FIELDING AVERAGES

					Test Career								
mat	inns	no	runs	hs	ave	bf	sr	100	50	4s	6s	ct	st
44	78	6	3245	260	45.06			8	13		3	16	0
					First-Class								
132	222	19	8916	263	43.92			16	51			68	1
					List A								
3	3	0	12	11	4.00			0	0			3	0

RIDLEY JACOBS
(Antigua)

Born November 26, 1967

Batting Style:
Left-hand bat

Ridley Jacobs' Test debut came against South Africa in 1998-99. Jacobs' relish for fast bowling helped him top the batting averages on that unhappy tour, and three years later he notched his maiden Test century against the same opponents in Barbados, and scored two more after that - the second of which kept England's bowlers away from the West Indian tail as Brian Lara went about scoring his 400. Given a true pitch, Jacobs could be compelling viewing, unleashing booming strokes off either foot from a high backlift, but quality spins tended to tie him in knots. His batting, if inelegant, became more consistent and he was a valuable source of runs for West Indies. However, his glovework started to fail him and his form fell away dramatically in England in 2004.

BATTING AND FIELDING AVERAGES

Test Career

mat	inns	no	runs	hs	ave	bf	sr	100	50	4s	6s	ct	st
65	112	21	2577	118	28.31	5391	47.80	3	14	300	23	207	12

One Day International

mat	inns	no	runs	hs	ave	bf	sr	100	50	4s	6s	ct	st
147	112	32	1865	80	23.31	2662	70.06	0	9	118	27	160	29

First-Class

mat	inns	no	runs	hs	ave	bf	sr	100	50	4s	6s	ct	st
157	251	57	7518	149	38.75			17	40			443	33

List A

mat	inns	no	runs	hs	ave	bf	sr	100	50	4s	6s	ct	st
222	175	51	3180	85	25.64			0	16			254	43

BERNARD JULIEN
(Trinidad)

Born March 13, 1950

Batting Style:
Right-hand bat

Bernard Julien had a bit of everything: flashing strokeplay, brilliant fielding, lively left-arm seamers from a strange, stiff-legged run; orthodox or unorthodox left-arm spin; and the ability to charm fans and females alike. He could play, but his career at the top was fitful, with only two centuries and one five-for in 24 Tests. His first hundred was a violent affair, at Lord's in 1973, when he added 231 for the seventh wicket with another handy allrounder, Garry Sobers.

BATTING AND FIELDING AVERAGES

Test Career

mat	inns	no	runs	hs	ave	bf	sr	100	50	4s	6s	ct	st
24	34	6	866	121	30.92			2	3		7	14	0

One Day International

mat	inns	no	runs	hs	ave	bf	sr	100	50	4s	6s	ct	st
12	8	2	86	26	14.33	148	58.10	0	0			4	0

First-class

mat	inns	no	runs	hs	ave	bf	sr	100	50	4s	6s	ct	st
195	272	36	5790	127	24.53			3	27			126	0

List A

mat	inns	no	runs	hs	ave	bf	sr	100	50	4s	6s	ct	st
115	95	16	1450	104	18.35			1	3			28	0

ALVIN KALLICHARRAN
(Guyana – then British Guiana)

Born March 21, 1949

**Batting Style:
Left-hand bat**

Alvin Isaac Kallicharran was a West Indian batsman who played from 1972 to 1981. His elegant, watchful batting style produced some substantial innings for a West Indian team very much in its formative years in the seventies. He was Wisden's Cricketer of the Year for 1973.

Though he was a talented batsman like many of his peers, Kallicharran only managed 4473 runs, but at an average of 44.43 in 66 matches, he demonstrated his capability. He was part of the 1979 team that won the Cricket World Cup. His highest innings was a score of 187 against England in the 1974 tour.

BATTING AND FIELDING AVERAGES

Test Career

mat	inns	no	runs	hs	ave	bf	sr	100	50	4s	6s	ct	st
66	109	10	4399	187	44.43			12	21		12	51	0

One Day International

31	28	4	826	78	34.41	1329	62.15	0	6			8	0

First-Class

505	834	86	32650	243	43.64			87	160			323	0

List A

383	363	36	11336	206	34.66			15	71			86	0

ROHAN KANHAI
(Guyana – then British Guiana)

Born December 26, 1935

Batting Style:
Right-hand bat

Rohan Bholalall Kanhai was a right-handed West Indian batsman in the late fifties, sixties and early seventies. He is considered a cricketing legend and rated as perhaps the best batsman among West Indian players of East Indian descent.

As a specialist batsman, Kanhai hit 6,227 runs in 79 Tests at a robust average of 47.53, with his highest score of 256 coming against India in a Test at Calcutta. When Kanhai retired, his batting average was the fifth-highest of all West Indian cricketers with more than 20 Tests. He was famous for his unorthodox shots, most notably the "falling hook" shot, in which he finished his follow through lying on his back.

BATTING AND FIELDING AVERAGES

mat	inns	no	runs	hs	ave	bf	sr	100	50	4s	6s	ct	st
					Test Career								
79	137	6	6227	256	47.53			15	28		23	50	0
					One Day International								
7	5	2	164	55	54.66	273	60.07	0	2	19	1	4	0
					First-class								
416	669	82	28774	256	49.01			83	120			320	7
					List A								
159	151	29	4769	126	39.09			7	26			70	1

BRIAN LARA
(Trinidad)

Born May 2, 1969

Batting Style:
Left-hand bat

Brian Charles Lara (nicknamed "The Prince of Port-of-Spain" or simply "The Prince") is acknowledged as one of the world's greatest batsmen, having several times topped the Test batting rankings and being the current world record holder for the highest individual innings score and the all-time leading run scorer in Test cricket.

Lara has shown an almost unparalleled ability to build massive innings, and holds several world records for high scoring. He has the highest individual score in both first-class cricket (501 not out for Warwickshire against Durham in 1994) and Test cricket (400 not out for the West Indies against England in 2004). He also holds the record for the highest total number of runs in a Test career, after overtaking Allan Border in November 2005. He is the only man to have reclaimed the Test record score, having scored 375 against England in 1994, a record that stood until Matthew Hayden's 380 against Zimbabwe in 2003. His 400 not out also made him the second player after Don Bradman to score two Test triple-centuries, and the second after Bill Ponsford to score two first-class quadruple-centuries. He has scored eight double centuries in Test cricket, second only to Bradman's twelve.

cont'd.

BATTING AND FIELDING AVERAGES

Test Career

mat	inns	no	runs	hs	ave	bf	sr	100	50	4s	6s	ct	st
131	232	6	11593	400	52.88	19753	60.51	34	48	1559	88	164	0

One Day International

| 287 | 278 | 31 | 10019 | 169 | 40.56 | 12643 | 79.24 | 19 | 61 | 1004 | 124 | 114 | 0 |

First-Class

| 259 | 437 | 11 | 21971 | 501 | 51.57 | | | 64 | 87 | | | 317 | 0 |

List A

| 416 | 399 | 42 | 14216 | 169 | 39.82 | | | 27 | 84 | | | 171 | 0 |

CLIVE LLOYD
(Guyana then British Guiana)

Born August 31, 1944

**Batting Style:
Left-hand bat**

Clive Lloyd was the crucial ingredient in the rise of West Indian cricket. He was a hard-hitting batsman and one of the most successful captains in history. He led the West Indies to the top of world cricket for two decades.

Clive Lloyd made his first-class debut as a left-hand middle-order batsman in the then British Guiana in 1963-64 and played for Haslingden in the Lancashire League in 1967. He was offered terms by Warwickshire before signing for Lancashire, making his debut for them in 1968, and winning his cap the following season.

Lloyd had already made his Test debut, against India at Mumbai (then Bombay) in December 1966, hitting 82 and 78 not out as he put on 102 runs with Sobers to win the match on a pitch helping the spinners. His first home Test also brought his first Test century, 118 against England in Trinidad that helped stave off defeat. Another century followed in the fourth Test of that series to confirm he was at home at the highest level. Touring Australia in 1968-69 he hit another Test century, at Brisbane, in his first Test against them.

cont'd.

BATTING AND FIELDING AVERAGES

	mat	inns	no	runs	hs	ave	bf	sr	100	50	4s	6s	ct	st
Test Career														
	110	175	14	7515	242	46.67			19	39		70	90	0
One Day International														
	87	69	19	1977	102	39.54	2434	81.22	1	11			39	0
First-Class														
	490	730	96	31232	242	49.26			79	172			377	0
List A														
	375	343	72	10915	134	40.27			12	69			146	0

DERYCK MURRAY
(Trinidad)

Born May 20, 1943

Batting Style:
Right-hand bat

Deryck Murray, a former captain of the West Indies cricket team, was a thoughtful, composed figure in the West Indies side for 17 years. It started when Frank Worrell entrusted the wicket-keeping position in England in 1963 to a diminutive boyish figure, barely out of his teens - and was rewarded with a record 24 victims. His keeping was compact, tidy and, bearing in mind some of his more exuberant successors, generally understated. Nowadays, when more runs are demanded of keepers, he might not have played as much as he did. But his batting was as dapper as his glovework. At Bombay in 1974-75 he made 91 and helped Clive Lloyd add 250 for the sixth wicket.

BATTING AND FIELDING AVERAGES

Test Career

mat	inns	no	runs	hs	ave	bf	sr	100	50	4s	6s	ct	st
62	96	9	1993	91	22.90			0	11		7	181	8

One Day International

mat	inns	no	runs	hs	ave	bf	sr	100	50	4s	6s	ct	st
26	17	5	294	61	24.50	468	62.82	0	2			37	1

First-Class

mat	inns	no	runs	hs	ave	bf	sr	100	50	4s	6s	ct	st
367	554	85	13292	166*	28.34			10	72			740	108

List A

mat	inns	no	runs	hs	ave	bf	sr	100	50	4s	6s	ct	st
144	112	30	1938	82	23.63			0	7			165	14

JUNIOR MURRAY
(Grenada)

Born January 29, 1968

Batting Style:
Right-hand bat

Junior Randalph Murray was one of the few Test players to emerge from the tiny island of Grenada.

BATTING AND FIELDING AVERAGES

mat	inns	no	runs	hs	ave	bf	sr	100	50	4s	6s	ct	st
					Test Career								
33	45	4	918	101	22.39	1670	54.97	1	3	102	6	99	3
					One Day International								
55	36	6	678	86	22.60	929	72.98	0	5	63	6	46	7
					First-Class								
147	249	30	6780	218	30.95			11	30			335	30
					List A								
120	94	13	1851	100	22.85			1	8			92	31

SEYMOUR NURSE
(Barbados)

Born November 10, 1933

Batting Style:
Right- hand bat

Seymour Nurse was a powerfully-built batsman. He was a middle-order strokemaker who didn't really establish himself until the 1966 West Indian tour of England, when he was 32. Nurse then passed 50 five times in as many Tests, and though he hammered 137 at Headingley, his best innings probably came at Trent Bridge, where he thumped a majestic 93 in trying circumstances. He was a Wisden Cricketer of the Year in 1967, and finished his Test career with a magnificent 258 at Christchurch in 1968-69.

BATTING AND FIELDING AVERAGES

					Test Career								
mat	inns	no	runs	hs	ave	bf	sr	100	50	4s	6s	ct	st
29	54	1	2523	258	47.60			6	10		11	21	0
					First-class								
141	235	19	9489	258	43.93			26	40			116	0
					List A								
6	6	1	246	102	49.20			1	1			2	0

PATRICK PATTERSON
(Jamaica)

Born September 15, 1961

Batting Style:
Right-hand bat

Balfour Patrick Patterson played for the West Indies cricket team in the 1980s and 1990s.

BATTING AND FIELDING AVERAGES

Test Career

mat	inns	no	runs	hs	ave	bf	sr	100	50	4s	6s	ct	st
28	38	16	145	21	6.59	404	35.89	0	0	18	0	5	0

One Day International

mat	inns	no	runs	hs	ave	bf	sr	100	50	4s	6s	ct	st
59	20	15	44	13	8.80	101	43.56	0	0	1	1	9	0

First-Class

mat	inns	no	runs	hs	ave	bf	sr	100	50	4s	6s	ct	st
161	164	58	618	29	5.83			0	0			32	0

List A

mat	inns	no	runs	hs	ave	bf	sr	100	50	4s	6s	ct	st
100	35	25	106	16	10.60			0	0			15	0

SONNY RAMADHIN
(Trinidad)

Born May 1, 1929

Batting Style:
Right-hand bat

Sonny Ramadhin was a West Indian cricketer and was the first (of many) West Indian cricketers of East Indian origin. He was Wisden's Cricketer of the Year for 1951.

BATTING AND FIELDING AVERAGES

						Test Career								
mat	inns	no	runs	hs	ave	bf	sr	100	50		4s	6s	ct	st
43	58	14	361	44	8.20			0	0			0	9	0
						First-class								
184	191	65	1092	44	8.66			0	0				38	0
						List A								
5	1	0	0	0	0.00			0	0	0		0	0	0

SIR VIV RICHARDS
(Antigua)

Born March 7, 1952

Batting Style:
Right-hand bat

Sir Isaac Vivian Alexander Richards was an extremely good attacking right-hand batsman, a good fielder, an occasional spin bowler, and a successful captain. Richards made his Test match debut for the West Indian cricket team in 1974 against India in Bangalore. He made an unbeaten 192 in the second Test of the same series in New Delhi.

In his Test career, he scored 8,540 runs in 121 Test matches at an average of 50.23 (including 24 centuries). He won 27 of 50 matches as a Test captain, and lost only 8. He is also the scorer of the fastest ever Test century. His highest innings of 291 is sixth on the list of the West Indies' highest individual scores.

In 1976 Richards scored 1710 runs at 90.00 with seven centuries in 11 Tests, both records to this day. Rather surprisingly, in six ODIs he played that calendar year he managed only 112 runs at 28.00.

In 2000, Richards was named by a 100-member panel of experts one of the five Wisden Cricketers of the Century.

BATTING AND FIELDING AVERAGES

Test Career

mat	inns	no	runs	hs	ave	bf	sr	100	50	4s	6s	ct	st
121	182	12	8540	291	50.23			24	45		84	122	0

One Day International

mat	inns	no	runs	hs	ave	bf	sr	100	50	4s	6s	ct	st
187	167	24	6721	189	47.00	7451	90.20	11	45			100	0

First-class

mat	inns	no	runs	hs	ave	bf	sr	100	50	4s	6s	ct	st
507	796	63	36212	322	49.40			114	162			464	1

List A

mat	inns	no	runs	hs	ave	bf	sr	100	50	4s	6s	ct	st
500	466	61	16995	189	41.96			26	109			238	0

RICHIE RICHARDSON
(Antigua)

Born January 12, 1962

Batting Style:
Right-hand bat

Richard Benjamin Richardson was a former captain of the West Indies cricket team.

After Viv Richards' Test match retirement, Richie took on the mantle as the captain of the West Indies. He captained the team 24 times winning 11 matches. In the 4 years of his captaincy, the West Indies only lost one series, versus Australia in 1995.

Richie played 86 Test matches until 1995 scoring 5,949 runs and 16 centuries. He was very successful against Australia, hitting 9 centuries against them, and scored his highest score of 194 against India in Guyana in 1989. He also played 224 One Day Internationals including 3 World Cups. Richardson's last international was the 1996 World Cup Semi Final defeat against Australia, where he resigned the position of captain.

BATTING AND FIELDING AVERAGES

Test Career

mat	inns	no	runs	hs	ave	bf	sr	100	50	4s	6s	ct	st
86	146	12	5949	194	44.39			16	27		23	90	0

One Day International

mat	inns	no	runs	hs	ave	bf	sr	100	50	4s	6s	ct	st
224	217	30	6248	122	33.41	9801	63.74	5	44			75	0

First-class

mat	inns	no	runs	hs	ave	bf	sr	100	50	4s	6s	ct	st
234	390	31	14618	194	40.71			37	68			207	0

List A

mat	inns	no	runs	hs	ave	bf	sr	100	50	4s	6s	ct	st
313	304	37	8458	122	31.67			6	59			92	0

LAWRENCE ROWE
(Jamaica)

Born January 8, 1949

Batting Style:
Right-hand bat

Lawrence George Rowe, also known as "Yagga", was an elegant right handed batsman described by Michael Holding, his team mate, as "the best batsman I ever saw". He made his debut for Jamaica in 1968-69. He then made history on his Test match debut v New Zealand at Kingston 1972 scoring 214 and 100 not out, the first time that a cricketer had scored a double and single century on a Test debut. Rowe was a heavy scorer at his home ground. In 1974 v England he scored 302 in 10 hours. Rowe was seen as a West Indies batting "hero" in the days before Viv Richards. He played 30 Test matches scoring a total of 2,047 runs at an average of 43. He was known to whistle whilst he batted though he seemed to be injury prone; he suffered problems with his eyesight and was allergic to grass. He played Tests between 1972 and 1980 and played 11 one-day internationals. Rowe played for Derbyshire in the English County Championship and also joined World Series Cricket. He is one of only four West Indian batsmen to have scored a triple century, the others being Garfield Sobers, Chris Gayle and Brian Lara.

BATTING AND FIELDING AVERAGES

Test Career

mat	inns	no	runs	hs	ave	bf	sr	100	50	4s	6s	ct	st
30	49	2	2047	302	43.55			7	7		6	17	0

One Day International

| 11 | 8 | 0 | 136 | 60 | 17.00 | 244 | 55.73 | 0 | 1 | | 0 | 2 | 0 |

First-class

| 149 | 245 | 12 | 8755 | 302 | 37.57 | | | 18 | 38 | | | 118 | 0 |

List A

| 52 | 48 | 2 | 1400 | 87 | 30.43 | | | 0 | 10 | | | 18 | 0 |

MARLON SAMUELS
(Jamaica)

Born January 5, 1981

Batting Style:
Right-hand bat

Marlon Nathaniel Samuels made his Test debut in Australia in 2000, and his one day international debut against Sri Lanka in Nairobi in the same year. When Samuels flew into Australia for the third Test of the 2000-01 series, he was only 19 and had yet to represent his native Jamaica in a first-class match.

BATTING AND FIELDING AVERAGES

mat	inns	no	runs	hs	ave	bf	sr	100	50	4s	6s	ct	st
Test Career													
23	41	4	1044	104	28.21	2332	44.76	1	7	142	5	9	0
One Day International													
79	73	13	1711	108	28.51	2346	72.93	2	10	178	21	22	0
First-class													
57	96	7	3168	257	35.59			5	20			31	0
List A													
128	119	21	3148	108	32.12			4	21			36	0
Twenty20													
2	2	1	57	32	57.00	32	178.12	0	0			0	0

RAMNARESH SARWAN
(Guyana)

Born June 23, 1980

Batting Style:
Right-hand bat

Ramnaresh Ronnie Sarwan has been a member of the West Indian cricket team since his Test debut against Pakistan at Barbados in May 2000 when he remained unbeaten in both innings scoring 84 in the first innings. He missed out on scoring his maiden Test century against South Africa in March 2001 when he was run out for 91. His score of 78 in the 2nd Test against India at Chennai in October 2002 was his 4th innings of 75+ that couldn't be converted into a century. His maiden Test century came in his next Test series against Bangladesh at Dhaka. His next Test century came against Australia at St. John's in May 2003. His best innings (261 not out) came against Bangladesh in June 2004. He has played 59 Test matches scoring at an average of 40 runs per innings with 6 centuries and 21 fifties.

cont'd.

BATTING AND FIELDING AVERAGES

Test Career

mat	inns	no	runs	hs	ave	bf	sr	100	50	4s	6s	ct	st
65	118	8	4268	261	38.80	9431	44.83	9	26	564	8	46	0

One Day International

| 115 | 107 | 23 | 3724 | 115 | 44.33 | 4849 | 76.79 | 3 | 24 | 314 | 36 | 33 | 0 |

First-class

| 156 | 266 | 19 | 9203 | 261 | 37.25 | | | 21 | 51 | | | 118 | 0 |

List A

| 173 | 163 | 30 | 5529 | 118 | 41.57 | | | 7 | 31 | | | 53 | 0 |

Twenty20

| 4 | 4 | 1 | 80 | 49 | 26.66 | 79 | 101.26 | 0 | 0 | | | 0 | 0 |

PHIL SIMMONS
(Trinidad)

Born April 18, 1963

Batting Style:
Right-arm bat

Phil Simmons was an explosive allrounder. His finest achievement was probably taking Leicestershire to the County Championship with a towering season in 1996, when he collected 1244 runs and 56 wickets, and 35 catches.

BATTING AND FIELDING AVERAGES

mat	inns	no	runs	hs	ave	bf	sr	100	50	4s	6s	ct	st
					Test Career								
26	47	2	1002	110	22.26	1933	51.83	1	4		4	26	0
					One Day International								
143	138	11	3675	122	28.93	5407	67.96	5	18			55	0
					First-class								
207	345	17	11682	261	35.61			24	65			241	0
					List A								
306	296	27	8929	166	33.19			12	54			137	0

COLLIE SMITH
(Jamaica)

Born May 5, 1933

Batting Style:
Right-hand bat

O'Neil Gordon 'Collie' Smith was a hard hitting batsman who was rated highly in the West Indies. He idolised Jim Laker for which reason he was nicknamed 'Jim' for a time. In his third first class match, he hit 169 for Jamaica against the touring Australians and was immediately included in the Test side. He started his Test career scoring 104 on debut against Australia. But after a 'pair' in the next match, he was dropped.

In England in 1957, he scored 161 and 168 in Test matches, once driving Brian Statham into the car park.

BATTING AND FIELDING AVERAGES

Test Career

mat	inns	no	runs	hs	ave	bf	sr	100	50	4s	6s	ct	st
26	42	0	1331	168	31.69			4	6		12	9	0

First-class

mat	inns	no	runs	hs	ave	bf	sr	100	50	4s	6s	ct	st
70	112	12	4031	169	40.31			10	20			39	0

SIR GARFIELD SOBERS
(Barbados)

Born July 28, 1936

Batting Style:
Left-hand bat

Sir Garfield St Auburn Sobers is universally regarded as one of the most exceptional players ever to grace the game. Sobers was a true all-rounder, he both batted and bowled, and was also an outstanding fielder, usually fielding close to the wicket. With the ball, Sobers performed superbly, taking 235 Test wickets at an average of 34.03. He bowled left-arm orthodox spin, left-arm unorthodox spin, and also left-arm fast-medium. Sobers was also exceptionally talented with the bat, with a career Test batting average of 57.78. He scored a then record 8032 runs in his career.

Sobers played his first Test match in 1953, aged only 17. Just under five years later, in 1958, Sobers set a Test cricket record by scoring 365 runs in 614 minutes, in a single innings that included 38 fours and, interestingly, not one six against Pakistan. It was his first Test century, and a record which stood for over 36 years. The record has since been surpassed twice by Brian Lara, also of the West Indies, who scored 375 and 400 not out in 1994 and 2004 respectively, and Matthew Hayden of Australia who scored 380 in 2003.

In 1968, Sobers became the first ever batsman to hit six

sixes off one over of six consecutive balls in first-class cricket. This tally of 36 runs off an over beat a 57 year-old record of 34 runs, held by Ted Alletson.

BATTING AND FIELDING AVERAGES

						Test Career							
mat	inns	no	runs	hs	ave	bf	sr	100	50	4s	6s	ct	st
93	160	21	8032	365	57.78			26	30		32	109	0
						One Day International							
1	1	0	0	0	0.00	6	0.00	0	0	0	0	1	0
						First-class							
383	609	93	28314	365	54.87			86	121			407	0
						List A							
95	92	21	2721	116	38.32			1		18		41	0

JEFFREY STOLLMEYER
(Trinidad)

Born March 11, 1921

Batting Style:
Right-hand bat

Jeffrey Stollmeyer was a considerable influence in West Indies cricket, both on and off the field, first during the days when whites controlled the game, and then in the transition to a more democratic process. Tall and graceful with a good range of strokes marked especially by the drive, he made his major impact on the international scene with his solid left-hand opening partner, Allan Rae, providing the base on which Weekes, Worrell and Walcott were to build so effectively on the 1950 tour of England. It was this series, won 3-1, that catapulted the West Indies into the top rank of Test teams.

BATTING AND FIELDING AVERAGES

Test Career

mat	inns	no	runs	hs	ave	bf	sr	100	50	4s	6s	ct	st
32	56	5	2159	160	42.33			4	12		3	20	0

CLYDE WALCOTT
(Barbados)

Born January 17, 1926

Batting Style:
Right-hand bat

A well-built and powerful batsman with a crouching stance, **Clyde Walcott** was a savage driver and cutter, but also possessed a solid defence when the need demanded. He first hit the headlines in 1945-46 when he added an unbroken 574 for the fourth wicket with schoolmate Frank Worrell for Barbados against Trinidad at Port-of-Spain - it remains the record West Indian stand for any wicket. He was 20.

Walcott was a member of the 'three W's', along with Everton Weekes and Frank Worrell, noted as outstanding batsmen from Barbados who all made their debut against England in 1948. In 1955, playing against Australia, Walcott became the first batsman to score five centuries in a single Test series, as he totalled 827 runs from 10 innings, including centuries in both innings of a match twice.

BATTING AND FIELDING AVERAGES

Test Career

mat	inns	no	runs	hs	ave	bf	sr	100	50	4s	6s	ct	st
44	74	7	3798	220	56.68			15	14			53	11

First-class

mat	inns	no	runs	hs	ave	bf	sr	100	50	4s	6s	ct	st
146	238	29	11820	314	56.55			40	54			174	33

EVERTON WEEKES
(Barbados)

Born February 26, 1925

Batting Style:
Right-hand bat

Sir Everton de Courcy Weekes was was a member of the 'three W's', along with Clyde Walcott and Frank Worrell, noted as outstanding batsmen from Barbados who all made their debut in 1948 against England. His most famous feat took place in 1948/1949, when he scored a Test-record five centuries in consecutive innings, and was run-out within ten runs of a sixth. These were Weekes' first five centuries, and this record still stands as of 2006.

Other notable achievements include three centuries in consecutive innings against New Zealand in 1956, a partnership of 338 with Frank Worrell against England in 1954, still a West Indian record for the third wicket in Tests, and a Knighthood for services to cricket in 1995.

BATTING AND FIELDING AVERAGES

Test Career

mat	inns	no	runs	hs	ave	bf	sr	100	50	4s	6s	ct	st
48	81	5	4455	207	58.61			15	19		2	49	0

First-class

mat	inns	no	runs	hs	ave	bf	sr	100	50	4s	6s	ct	st
152	241	24	12010	304	55.34			36	54			124	1

FRANK WORRELL
(Barbados)

Born August 1, 1924

Batting Style:
Right-hand bat

Sir Frank was a man of strong convictions, a brave man and it goes without saying, a great cricketer. Though he made his name as a player his greatest contribution was to destroy for ever the myth that a coloured cricketer was not fit to lead a team. Once appointed, he ended the cliques and rivalries between the players of various islands to weld together a team which in the space of five years became the champions of the world.

He was a man of true political sense and feeling, a federalist who surely would have made even greater contributions to the history of the West Indies had he not died so tragically in hospital of leukaemia at the early age of 42, a month after returning from India.

BATTING AND FIELDING AVERAGES

Test Career

mat	inns	no	runs	hs	ave	bf	sr	100	50	4s	6s	ct	st
51	87	9	3860	261	49.48			9	22		11	43	0

First-class

mat	inns	no	runs	hs	ave	bf	sr	100	50	4s	6s	ct	st
208	326	49	15025	308	54.24			39	80			139	0

HONOURABLE MENTION

*The following batsmen did not meet the criteria
(at least 20 Tests) but have had an impact
on the game.*

JOEY CAREW
(Trinidad)

Born September 15, 1937

Batting Style:
Left-hand bat

Michael Conrad "Joey" Carew is a former West Indian cricketer who played in 19 Tests from 1963 to 1972. An attractive left-hand opener who struck the ball cleanly, notably through the covers off the back foot, "Joey" Carew impressed in two matches against MCC in 1959-60, and made three tours of England and one to Australia. He was not an overall success in English conditions, though he managed 677 runs in 12 matches in 1969, despite a damaged finger. His best season in representative cricket was 1968-69. Carew was a mentor to a young Brian Lara at the beginning of Lara's career.

BATTING AND FIELDING AVERAGES

Test Career

mat	inns	no	runs	hs	ave	bf	sr	100	50	4s	6s	ct	st
19	36	3	1127	109	34.15			1	5		1	13	0

First-class

mat	inns	no	runs	hs	ave	bf	sr	100	50	4s	6s	ct	st
129	221	18	7810	182	38.47			13	43			83	0

List A

mat	inns	no	runs	hs	ave	bf	sr	100	50	4s	6s	ct	st
2	2	0	113	78	56.50			0	1			0	0

MAURICE FOSTER
(Jamaica)

Born May 9, 1943

Batting Style:
Right-hand bat

Maurice Foster was a solid middle-order batsman and who was one of the Shell Shield's most prolific runscorers in the late 60s and early 70s. He made his Test debut against England on West Indies 1969 tour, but enjoyed his best series against Australia in 1972-73 when he averaged 43.67. He only passed fifty once in that series, but his 125 in front of his home crowd at Kingston was his only Test hundred - he had made 99 two years earlier against New Zealand. He toured England for a second time in 1973, only playing in the innings victory at Lord's (the only time he was on the winning side in 14 Tests) but thereafter his appearances were increasingly spasmodic as a new generation of batsmen emerged.

cont'd.

BATTING AND FIELDING AVERAGES

Test Career

mat	inns	no	runs	hs	ave	bf	sr	100	50	4s	6s	ct	st
14	24	5	580	125	30.52			1	1		0	3	0

ODIs

mat	inns	no	runs	hs	ave	bf	sr	100	50	4s	6s	ct	st
2	1	0	25	25	25.00	62	40.32	0	0	4	0	0	0

First-class

mat	inns	no	runs	hs	ave	bf	sr	100	50	4s	6s	ct	st
112	175	26	6731	234	45.17			17	35			36	0

List A

mat	inns	no	runs	hs	ave	bf	sr	100	50	4s	6s	ct	st
9	8	1	151	49	21.57			0	0			4	0

DAVID MURRAY
(Barbados)

Born May 29, 1950

Batting Style:
Right-hand bat

David Murray was a talented wicketkeeper and a capable batsman who made three Test fifties and a first-class double hundred, at Jamshedpur on the 1978-79 tour of India. He took over from Deryck Murray - they were not related - in 1980-81 and was briefly No. 1. He was banned from cricket in the West Indies after playing in South Africa, and his last Test appearance came at Sydney in 1981-82.

BATTING AND FIELDING AVERAGES

Test Career

mat	inns	no	runs	hs	ave	bf	sr	100	50	4s	6s	ct	st
19	31	3	601	84	21.46			0	3		0	57	5

ODIs

mat	inns	no	runs	hs	ave	bf	sr	100	50	4s	6s	ct	st
10	7	2	45	35	9.00	131	34.35	0	0	6	0	16	0

First-class

mat	inns	no	runs	hs	ave	bf	sr	100	50	4s	6s	ct	st
114	176	30	4503	206	30.84			7	19			293	30

List A

mat	inns	no	runs	hs	ave	bf	sr	100	50	4s	6s	ct	st
49	37	11	627	78	24.11			0	4			68	3

ALLAN RAE
(Jamaica)

Born September 30, 1922

Batting Style:
Left-hand bat

Allan Fitzroy Rae, who died on February 27, 2005, at age 82, was a lefthanded opening batsman whose century for West Indies at Lord's in 1950 helped change the face of cricket. Rae scored a dogged 106 to set the stage for the team's strokemakers and spinners who secured one of the game's most famous victories. He scored heavily in the West Indies' two subsequent wins, including another hundred at The Oval.

BATTING AND FIELDING AVERAGES

Test Career

mat	inns	no	runs	hs	ave	bf	sr	100	50	4s	6s	ct	st
15	24	2	1016	109	46.18			4	4		4	10	0

First-class

mat	inns	no	runs	hs	ave	bf	sr	100	50	4s	6s	ct	st
80	128	7	4798	179	39.65			17	15			42	0

FAMOUS PLAYERS

- 1920s: Learie Constantine

- 1930s: George Headley, Manny Martindale

- 1940s: Clyde Walcott, Everton Weekes, Frank Worrell (collectively known as the Three W's)

- 1950s: Basil Butcher, Lance Gibbs, Wes Hall, Conrad Hunte, Rohan Kanhai, Sonny Ramadhin, Garry Sobers, Alfred Valentine

- 1960s: Charlie Griffith, Vanburn Holder, Clive Lloyd, Seymour Nurse

- 1970s: Colin Croft, Joel Garner, Larry Gomes, Gordon Greenidge, Desmond Haynes, Michael Holding, Alvin Kallicharran, Malcolm Marshall, Viv Richards, Andy Roberts, Lawrence Rowe

- 1980s: Curtly Ambrose, Ian Bishop, Jeff Dujon, Carl Hooper, Richie Richardson, Courtney Walsh

- 1990s: Jimmy Adams, Shivnarine Chanderpaul, Mervyn Dillon, Brian Lara

- 2000s: Ramnaresh Sarwan, Chris Gayle

TEST CAPTAINS

No.	Name	Period
1	Karl Nunes	1928-1929/30
2	Teddy Hoad	1929/30
3	Nelson Betancourt	1929/30
4	Maurice Fernandes	1929/30
5	Jackie Grant1	1930/31-1934/35
6	Rolph Grant1	1939
7	George Headley	1947/48
8	Gerry Gomez	1947/48
9	John Goddard	1947/48-1951/52, 1957
10	Jeffrey Stollmeyer	1951/52-1954/55
11	Denis Atkinson	1954/55-1955/56
12	Gerry Alexander	1957/58-1959/60
13	Frank Worrell	1960/61-1963
14	Garfield Sobers	1964/65-1971/72
15	Rohan Kanhai	1972/73-1973/74
16	Clive Lloyd	1974/75-1977/78, 1979/80-1984/85
17	Alvin Kallicharran	1977/78-1978/79
18	Deryck Murray	1979/80
19	Viv Richards	1980, 1983/84-1991
20	Gordon Greenidge	1987/88
21	Desmond Haynes	1989/90-1990/91
22	Richie Richardson	1991/92-1995
23	Courtney Walsh	1993/94-1997/98
24	Brian Lara	1996/97-1999/2000,2002/03-2004, 2006-present

25	Jimmy Adams	1999/2000-2000/01
26	Carl Hooper	2000/01-2002/03
27	Ridley Jacobs	2002/03
28	Shivnarine Chanderpaul	2004/05-2005/06

WEST INDIES SQUAD 2006

Shivnarine Chanderpaul

Ramnaresh Sarwan

Chris Gayle

Devon Smith

Brian Lara

Daren Ganga

Denesh Ramdin

Dwayne Bravo

Dwayne Smith

Wavell Hinds

Runako Morton

Daren Powell

Fidel Edwards

Jerome Taylor

Ian Bradshaw

Deighton Butler

Rawl Lewis